Ballet

Caroline Plaisted

Carnegie Primary
School

OXFORD
UNIVERSITY PRESS

Contents

Introduction

On Mondays we go to our ballet class.

Stretching

First, we sit on the floor.

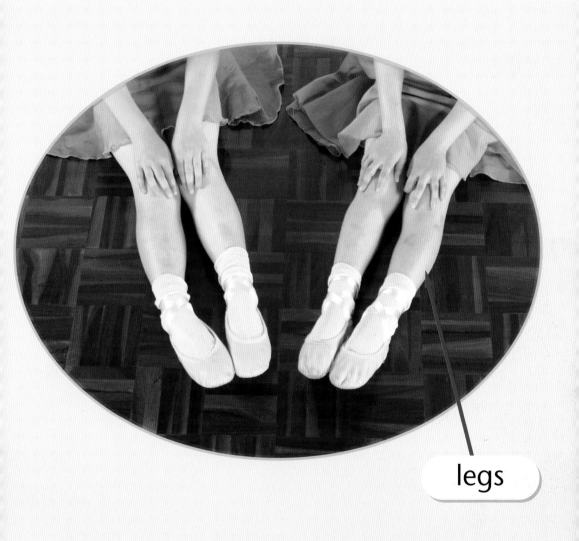

legs

We stretch out our legs in front.

Bending

We stand up to do knee bends.

knee

down

up

I bend down to the music.
Then I pull myself up again.

Jumping

I love to jump in my ballet class.
I go up and down to the music.

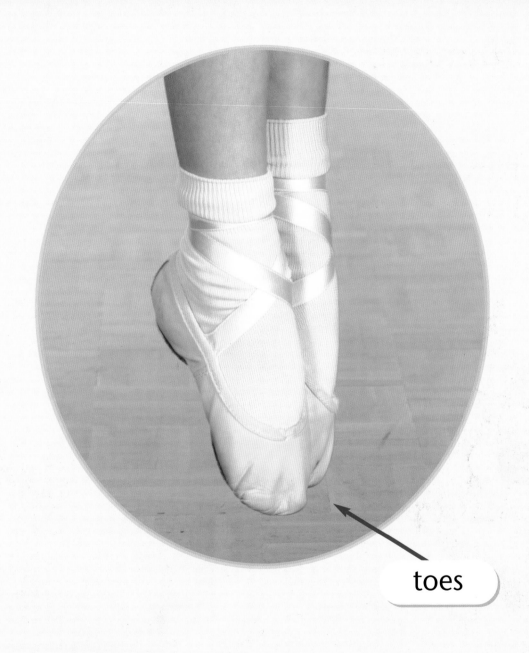

toes

I point my toes when I go up.

Skipping

Then we skip across the room.

I go first.

Dancing in a line

Next we all dance in a line.
We all hold hands.

arm

hands

left foot

We point with one foot.

right foot

Then we point with the other foot.

Dancing around

We swirl and twirl to the music.

I love to dance at my ballet class.

Index